Nuclear Energy
Power from the Atom

Troon Harrison Adams

Crabtree Publishing Company
www.crabtreebooks.com

Crabtree Publishing Company
www.crabtreebooks.com

Author: Troon Harrison Adams
Editor: Lynn Peppas
Proofreader: Crystal Sikkens
Editorial director: Kathy Middleton
Production coordinator: Amy Salter
Prepress technician: Amy Salter
Produced by: Plan B Book Packagers
Developed and produced by: Plan B Book Packagers

Photographic plate made by Henri Becquerel: p. 12 (bottom)
Shutterstock: Kletr: cover; Martin D. Vonka: p. 1; 2265524729:
p. 4; Arvydas Kniukšta: p. 5; Ilja Mašík: p. 6 (top); Saasemen:
p. 6 (bottom); Leong Yoke Shu: p. 7 (right); Tonis Valing:
p. 7 (left); Steve Estvanik: p. 8 (top); Thoron: p. 8 (bottom);
Stephen Finn: p. 9 (bottom); Losevsky Pavel: p. 9 (top); T.W.
Van Urk: p. 10; Dalis: p. 11 (top); Darren Baker: p. 11 (bottom);

Ken Brown: p. 12 (middle); Stocksnapp: p. 12 (top); Rainer
Villido: p. 13; Steve Shoup: p. 14; Neale Cousland: p. 15; John
Carnemolla: p. 16; Justin Paget: p. 17 (bottom); Petr Vaclavek:
p. 17 (top); Andrea Danti: p. 18; Vibrant Image Studio: p. 19;
Sergey Kamshylin: p. 20; Rafa Irusta: p. 21 (top); Magnola:
p. 21 (bottom); Joyfull: p. 22; Sergey Kamshylin: p. 23; CROM:
p. 24; Dimos: p. 25 (top); Melvin Lee: p. 25 (bottom); Artshots:
p. 26; Darren Brode: p. 27 (bottom); Maxp: p. 27 (middle);
Monkey Business Images: p. 27 (top); Kaleb Madsen: p. 28; Paul
McKinnon: p. 29; Sergey Kamshylin: p. 30 (bottom); Dan Simonsen:
p. 30 (top); Bezikus: p. 31 (bottom); Pincasso: p. 31 (top)

Cover: Agricultural land surrounds the cooling towers of
the Temelin nuclear power plant in the Czech Republic.

Title page: A nuclear power station's cooling towers.

Library and Archives Canada Cataloguing in Publication

Harrison, Troon, 1958-
      Nuclear energy power from the atom / Troon Harrison Adams.

(Energy revolution)
Includes index.
ISBN 978-0-7787-2921-1 (bound).--ISBN 978-0-7787-2935-8 (pbk.)

1. Nuclear energy--Juvenile literature.
I. Title. II. Series: Energy revolution

TK9148.H37 2010   j333.792'4   C2009-906926-1

Library of Congress Cataloging-in-Publication Data

Adams, Troon Harrison.
   Nuclear energy power from the atom / Troon Harrison Adams.
      p. cm. -- (Energy revolution)
   Includes index.
   ISBN 978-0-7787-2935-8 (pbk. : alk. paper) -- ISBN 978-0-7787-2921-1
(reinforced library binding : alk. paper)
   1. Nuclear energy--Juvenile literature. 2. Atoms--Juvenile literature. 3.
Nuclear energy. 4. Atoms. I. Title. II. Series.

   QC778.5.A37 2010
   333.792'4--dc22

                                                         2009048030

Crabtree Publishing Company

Printed in the U.S.A./122009/CG20091120

www.crabtreebooks.com   1-800-387-7650

Published in Canada
Crabtree Publishing
616 Welland Ave.
St. Catharines, ON
L2M 5V6

Published in the United States
Crabtree Publishing
PMB 59051
350 Fifth Avenue, 59th Floor
New York, New York 10118

Published in the United Kingdom
Crabtree Publishing
Maritime House
Basin Road North, Hove
BN41 1WR

Published in Australia
Crabtree Publishing
386 Mt. Alexander Rd.
Ascot Vale (Melbourne)
VIC 3032

Contents

Energy Conservation: "We Can Do It!"

"We Can Do It" was a slogan that appeared on posters made during World War II. One poster featured "Rosie the Riveter," a woman dressed in blue coveralls (shown below). The poster was originally intended to encourage women to enter the workforce in industry to replace the men who left to serve in the war. Today, the image of Rosie the Riveter represents a time when people came together as a society to reach a common goal. Today's energy challenge can be combatted in a similar way. Together, we can work to save our planet from the pollution caused by burning **fossil fuels** by learning to conserve energy and developing alternative energy sources.

We Can Do It!

WAR PRODUCTION CO-ORDINATING COMMITTEE

Full of Energy

Everything that happens around you requires energy. Heat, movement, and noise are kinds of energy. Reading this book requires energy that your body makes from food. Without energy, the world would be silent, dark, and still.

What is Energy?

Energy contains the power to transform objects and to sustain life. Energy cannot be destroyed but it can move from one object to another. When energy transfers between objects, it can make them move. When a person paddles a canoe, the energy stored in their body helps the canoe move.

Energy Users

Humans have always wanted more energy than is in their own bodies. Many years ago, horses were harnessed to wagons to make them move. Today, cars move by harnessing the energy found in gas. Fossil fuels, including coal, oil, and gas, power and move many forms of machinery and transportation. In industries, fossil fuels provide energy for **chemical** changes, and to create synthetic and **petrochemical** materials such as plastic. It is believed the world demand for energy will almost double by 2050.

A kayaker uses the energy stored in his body to direct his craft. The energy of rushing water propels, or drives, him forward.

Infinite Energy

Fossil fuels that people harness for energy are **finite** and will run out because there is a limited supply. Societies need to find ways to use the energy contained in **infinite** sources, such as the Sun, wind, and water. These sources contain the power to make things move and change, but will never run out. Plant energy is renewable because new plants can be grown to replace those that have been harvested.

Sailing ships harness the energy of wind to move. Wind is infinite, or endless, and is known as a renewable energy source.

Conservation Tip

When you leave a room, switch off the light! Electric lights consume about 15 percent of the total energy used in a house, but you can help to make that number lower. Using more efficient bulbs also cuts down on electricity use and lowers the bill.

Fossil Fuel Addiction

Societies worldwide depend upon fossil fuels for travel, for farm machinery to plant and harvest crops, and for making a wide range of industrial and consumer products. Energy from fossil fuels heats and cools buildings. It provides electricity to run tools and appliances. Life would be very different if fossil fuels no longer existed.

Where in the World?

Currently, about one-eighth of the world's oil is produced in Saudi Arabia. There might only be enough oil there to last another 50 to 80 years. In the United States, the largest oil field discovered in 100 years is in Prudhoe Bay, Alaska, but only contains enough oil to last for a few years. Americans consume over 20 million barrels of oil per day.

Humans burn fossil fuels for energy to heat and cool houses and to power automobiles. Burning fossil fuels harms the environment.

Fueling the World

Fossil fuels formed underground through millions of years by the decay and **compression** of dead plants and animals. These raw fuels must be mined, or extracted, using heavy equipment that can cause environmental damage and contaminate **watersheds**. After being extracted, fossil fuels are transported by pipelines, ships, trucks, and trains. Gas pipelines can disrupt the migration patterns of animals, and spills of oil at sea can kill marine life. Extracting and transporting fossil fuels itself requires the **consumption** of large quantities of fuel and causes pollution. Fossil fuels have to be processed or refined, and this too uses energy.

Drilling, digging, and processing fossil fuels is expensive. It also takes a lot of energy to make fossil fuel energy.

A white swan's feathers are smudged in oil from an oil spill that polluted its habitat.

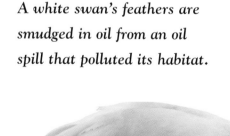

7

Under Threat

It is important to conserve fossil fuels because supplies are dwindling. They also pollute Earth's **atmosphere** with carbon dioxide, methane, and other **greenhouse gases**. These carbon emissions, or discharges, contribute to global warming. Thirty percent of carbon dioxide emissions in the United States come from transportation, and another 40 percent come from electric power plants.

Global warming is causing climate change. Scientists believe melting ice at the Earth's poles will cause sea levels to rise as much as 50 inches (127 cm) by 2100.

Global Warming Threat

Global warming is a problem with serious consequences. It is the gradual rise of Earth's temperature that is leading to the destruction of habitats, animals, and human life. Scientists believe it is caused largely by the burning of fossil fuels and the discharge of excess carbon into the environment. Earth is heated by the Sun's rays or energy. Some of this heat escapes back into space through the layers of atmosphere surrounding the planet. Greenhouse gases such as carbon dioxide and nitrous oxide occur naturally in the atmosphere and are necessary to keep the planet warm enough to live on.

When we create excess greenhouse gases by burning fossil fuels, too much heat is trapped in the atmosphere, contributing to a rise in temperatures.

Global warming is melting glaciers at an alarming rate.

Acid Rain

Acid rain is caused by burning fossil fuels which release sulfur dioxide and nitrogen oxide. In the atmosphere, these gases react with oxygen and other chemicals to form acids that change rain water. Acid rain falls into lakes and rivers, harming water plants and animals. If a body of water is severely affected, all life in it dies. In the United States, approximately two-thirds of sulfur dioxide and one-quarter of nitrogen oxide comes from fossil fuels, particularly coal, being burned to generate electricity. Automobile emissions also contribute to acid rain. Wind can carry emissions hundreds of miles to cause acid rain in wilderness areas.

CASE STUDY

London: Fewer cars = cleaner air

Congestion charging

C

Central ZONE

Mon - Fri 7 am - 6:30 pm

Since 2003, the city of London, England, has said no to idling car engines and traffic congestion. Before 2003, 250,000 vehicles entered central London every day on 25 traffic lanes. These vehicles spent about 50 percent of their time in traffic jams with engines idling. In 2003, London's mayor brought in a plan to decrease the number of cars by requiring drivers to pay a fee, or toll. Millions of dollars were collected and put into public transportation which ran more efficiently due to the decrease in traffic congestion. As a result, 85 percent of people entering the toll area today ride on public transportation, and the use of bicycles has increased. There are fewer cars on the roads and they move faster, spending less time idling their engines in gridlock. There has also been a 30 percent drop in congestion, and a 20 percent decrease in fossil fuel consumption and carbon emissions. Cities in North America, including San Francisco and New York, are currently studying the possibility of introducing similar plans.

Energy Alternatives

Fossil fuels account for so much of the world's energy that it will take many different energy sources to replace them. Some of these sources are renewable. Some have great potential for the future.

Nuclear Alternative?

Some people consider nuclear energy an alternative energy source but it is not a renewable resource like wind power, solar power, biomass, or hydropower. It depends upon mining a mineral called uranium. Eventually, the world's supply will run out. Currently, nuclear power plants generate about 17 percent of the world's energy, and the United States is the leading producer of nuclear energy. Nuclear plants are able to produce huge amounts of energy from small amounts of raw material. They produce less greenhouse gases and for this reason, present an alternative energy source.

Biomass

Biomass includes plant materials burned to generate electricity. Corn and sugar cane can be made into ethanol to fuel vehicles. In Brazil, about 50 percent of transportation is fueled by ethanol. The World Energy Council calls biomass "potentially the world's largest and most sustainable energy source." Some environmentalists say that although biomass fuels are better for the environment, they use up a lot of farm land that could be used to produce food for people.

Wind Power

Wind power uses giant wind **turbines** that can be built on any type of land and even at sea. They harness the energy of wind to power electrical generating stations. Electricity from wind is cheaper than electricity made from new coal or nuclear plants.

Sheep graze near a seaside wind farm. Wind farms can be located almost anywhere there is a lot of wind.

Power from the Sun

Wind power works well with solar power. On calm, sunny days, when windmills are not turning, solar panels mounted on rooftops, collect energy. A facility that combines power from wind and solar sources can be more reliable than other forms of power generating stations. In **developing nations**, where electricity lines have not been installed, solar panels provide readily available and often cheap electricity.

Hydropower

Hydroelectricity is power made from the energy in moving water. In many areas of the world, hydropower is created by damming rivers. In Norway, 99 percent of the country's electric power is created by hydroelectric power dams. Canada is the world's largest producer of hydroelectric power. Sixty percent of the country's electric power is from hydro.

High Tide

Tidal power and geothermal energy are other alternative energy sources that have great potential. In England, experts believe tidal power could one day supply one-fifth of the country's electricity. Plans for the future include building dams across tidal **estuaries**, and creating tide farms with turbines that work like underwater windmills. Geothermal energy uses heat from Earth and is generated in 24 countries around the world.

Iceland's geothermal "fields" and geysers have provided heat and power to the country since the 1930s.

Geothermal heat is piped from its source to power plants.

Conservation Tip

Try living without television or video games for a week. Flat screen televisions use more energy than refrigerators, microwaves, and stoves combined.

The Atomic Age

Scientists have been experimenting with uranium for hundreds of years. It was not until 1896, that French **physicist** Henri Becquerel accidentally discovered that uranium gave off invisible rays of energy. Scientist Marie Curie called these rays radiation. Curie used an **electrometer** invented by her husband Pierre, to determine that uranium caused the air around it to conduct electricity. She determined that radiation came from the uranium **atom** itself. Marie and Pierre Curie and Henri Becquerel were awarded the Nobel Prize in **physics** in 1903 for their research on radiation.

Lab Work

In 1905, physicist Albert Einstein announced a new **theory** that changed the way people understood energy. His theory was stated in the equation $E=mc2$, where E stands for energy and m stands for mass (the weight of an object). Einstein suggested that a small amount of mass could yield huge amounts of energy. Einstein's theory was confirmed in 1939. German chemists Otto Hahn and Fritz Strassmann, working with physicist Lise Meitner in Sweden, did experiments with uranium. In their experiments, some of the uranium atoms fissioned, or split, and this transformation released huge amounts of energy from a small amount of mass. Meitner's nephew, physicist Otto Frisch, replicated their experiments in 1939, and called the process "nuclear fission."

Einstein is known as one of the world's greatest scientists.

Marie Curie died of cancer caused by exposure to radiation. Today, we know that radiation can be deadly.

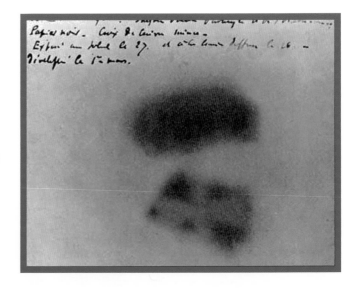

Henri Becquerel's plate with notes, used to discover that uranium gave off radiation energy.

A fence and warning signs surround the test site of the world's first nuclear weapons in New Mexico.

Nuclear Research

Italian physicist Enrico Fermi is known today as one of the greatest scientists of the last 100 years. In his lab, Fermi produced the first successful nuclear chain reaction in 1942. This generated enough energy through nuclear fission to power a flashlight bulb. Fermi was awarded a Nobel Prize in 1938 for his work in physics. He moved to the United States the next year and was part of a team which conducted the first nuclear fission experiments in the U.S. Fermi's research in nuclear energy as a power source led to the creation of the world's first artificial nuclear reactor. His work and that of other early nuclear scientists was also used in the creation of the world's first atomic bomb, a nuclear weapon that released vast quantities of energy from small amounts of **matter**.

What is Physics?

Physics is a branch of science that studies matter and energy, and the interactions between the two. Many physicists have worked on nuclear fission research since the 1930s. Physicists worked on nuclear weapons programs during World War II and nuclear energy programs after the war. The Atomic Age is the term given to the period of nuclear research that began with the first nuclear weapons tests in the New Mexico desert in July 1945. Soon after, the world's first nuclear bomb was detonated over Hiroshima, Japan in August 1945.

Tourists examine a replica Fat Man bomb made from plutonium 239 by the Manhattan Project. Fat Man was dropped over Nagasaki, Japan, on August 9, 1945. An earlier atom bomb, called Little Boy, was dropped over the city of Hiroshima on August 6, 1945. They were the only nuclear bombs ever dropped during war.

The Manhattan Project

When America joined in World War II, it was feared Germany was close to developing a powerful atomic bomb that depended on nuclear fission. American physicist J. Robert Oppenheimer, Nobel Prize winning physicists Neils Bohr, Enrico Fermi, and many other top scientists worked on The Manhattan Project, a secret effort to beat the Germans to this breakthrough. The first American atom bomb was tested in New Mexico in July 1945, after the war with Germany ended. One month later, two bombs were dropped on Hiroshima and Nagasaki, Japan, causing hundreds of thousands of deaths instantly, and ending the war in Japan. In the years following, many nations developed the capability to produce an atomic bomb and nuclear weapons. Global fears about mass destruction grew throughout this period known as the Cold War. In 1954, U.S. President Dwight Eisenhower delivered a famous speech, titled *Atoms For Peace*. He urged countries to use nuclear fission for peaceful purposes and cooperate to monitor this energy source.

The Hiroshima Peace Memorial, or Genbaku Dome, is a building close to ground zero of the Hiroshima atomic bomb. Its ruin was preserved as an example of the horrible destructive power of nuclear weaponry.

After the Bomb

In the years after the war, the United States created the Atomic Energy Commission to direct nuclear research into nuclear energy possibilities. New reactors were built to create nuclear powered electricity. By 1991, the United States had more operating nuclear power plants than any country in the world. About 22 percent of the country's electricity was produced through nuclear power.

CASE STUDY

A Nuclear Power First

The U.S. Atomic Energy Commission, created in 1945, chose a remote site in Idaho to establish a National Reactor Testing Station (NERT). In 1955, electrical power from its uranium reactor was fed into the power lines of the town of Arco for over one hour. Arco became the first town in the world to receive electricity from atomic energy in a test designed to show that this new power source was safe. In 1961, NERT had a reactor meltdown and three people died in the world's first reactor accident. Today, experimental stations test reactors for U.S. Navy ships and seek new methods of dealing with nuclear waste.

Nuclear Know-How

Generating electricity from uranium begins with mining. Uranium is a mineral and an **element**. It was discovered in 1789 and is often found in a rock called pitchblende. Canada, Australia, Russia, and African countries including Niger and Namibia, are all sources of uranium. Deposits close to the surface are extracted in open-pit mines while deeper deposits are mined with shafts. Mines disrupt the surrounding habitat and expose miners to radiation. Radiation causes diseases such as cancer.

Yellow Cake

The uranium **ore** taken from the ground is crushed in large mills and the uranium is extracted using strong acid or alkali. Once dry, the uranium is known as yellow cake. It contains mainly an isotope, or form, of uranium called U-238. This is not as useful for making nuclear fission occur. The uranium undergoes an **enrichment** process to increase the isotope U-235 from one percent to four percent. The U-235 is the form of uranium needed for nuclear reactors because it is unstable and contains atoms that will split apart when bombarded with neutrons.

An open pit uranium mine. Uranium is a chemical element. The world's supply of uranium is expected to last another 100 years.

16

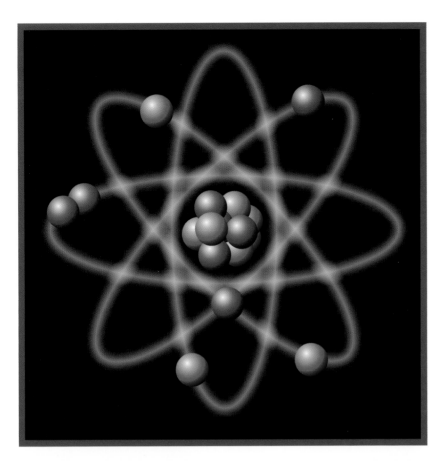

What is an Atom?

Atoms are particles contained in all matter. Every single thing in the world is composed of atoms too small to be seen under a powerful electron microscope. The atoms found in uranium will transform, or decay, into other types of atoms. This change from one type of atom (uranium) to other types of atoms (thorium and radium) is a process that occurs naturally and creates energy called radiation. This atomic change can also be forced to occur, and this is what happens inside a nuclear reactor.

Nuclear terms

Many words or sayings common in the English language have their origins in nuclear age research and technology. The phrases "going nuclear" or "having a meltdown" is sometimes used to describe someone who is really angry and about to "blow up." Nuclear explosions are extremely powerful and "nuclear meltdown" is a slang term for a severe nuclear accident. "Critical mass" is a term that describes a nuclear chain reaction and the smallest amount of material needed to reach it. The term "ground zero" is used to describe the point on Earth's surface where an explosion occured. The term was first used during work on the Manhattan Project. For a long time after World War II, the words ground zero meant the spot in Hiroshima, Japan, below where the nuclear bomb exploded.

Watch out! She is having a meltdown.

Fission

All atoms are composed of electrons circling a central core called a nucleus. A nucleus contains even tinier material called protons and neutrons. In a nuclear power station, the nucleus of an atom is split apart by bombarding the atom with a steady stream of neutrons. When the atom splits, in a process called nuclear fission, it releases radiation and heat. The amount of heat released by one atom is small, but nuclear reactors use the chain reaction that Fermi discovered. The atom splits and releases two or three neutrons that collide with other atoms and split them apart. This process continues until millions of neutrons and atoms collide, and millions of splits occur. A great deal of heat energy is generated.

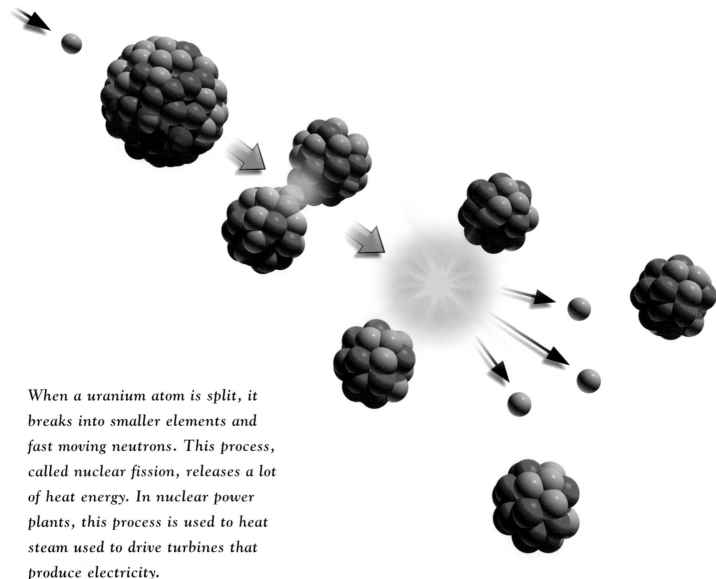

When a uranium atom is split, it breaks into smaller elements and fast moving neutrons. This process, called nuclear fission, releases a lot of heat energy. In nuclear power plants, this process is used to heat steam used to drive turbines that produce electricity.

Fusion

The opposite of nuclear fission is nuclear fusion. This occurs when the nuclei of two atoms combine to form one atom. Fission involves splitting and fusion involves joining. Both processes release heat energy. Our galaxy's Sun, and all other stars in our solar system, produce heat and light through the process of nuclear fusion. The Sun's energy is created by the fusion of the nuclei of hydrogen atoms. This creates the nucleus of a helium atom, and the energy produced takes only eight minutes to reach Earth.

Fusion Power?

Nuclear scientists are studying whether nuclear fusion could be used to generate power for human consumption. The fusion of one pound (0.45 kg) of nuclei produced more energy than burning 40 million pounds (18 million kg) of coal. Test reactors called Tokamaks have been built in Australia, England, and Italy. A fusion station in France might begin operation in 2016 but so far, all fusion sites are experimental.

CASE STUDY

Radiation Danger

Radiation consists of tiny particles that are subatomic (smaller than atoms) including neutrons and electrons. These travel through space at around 100,000 miles (160,934 km) per second. If they penetrate a body in large quantities, they damage cells and tissue. If a human is exposed to radiation, through a nuclear bomb or an accident at a nuclear plant, radiation poisoning results. This causes various cancers, and damage to reproductive organs. In 1954, America tested a new bomb, code named Castle Bravo, in the Pacific. It resulted in an explosion twice as large as expected. The wind carried the radioactive particles, called fallout, across populated islands. Although the islanders were evacuated, many suffered from radiation burns, and later from cancers and birth defects. A crew member on a Japanese fishing boat also died from radiation sickness which includes vomiting, hair loss, fever, dizzyness, and eventually loss of consciousness.

A Nuclear Power Plant

The world's first nuclear generating station opened at Calder Hall, England, in 1956. Today, there are over 400 nuclear reactors around the globe, supplying about 17 percent of the world's electricity. When fossil fuels are burned to produce electricity, their heat is used to create steam that turns turbines. These turbines generate an electrical charge. In nuclear plants, the splitting of atoms creates heat and steam to turn the turbines.

Cooling towers cool condensed steam from the nuclear generation process.

Location, location...

Due to the need for plentiful water supplies, nuclear reactors are often near coastlines. Rising sea levels might make site selection difficult. Another consideration is the stability of the ground. An earthquake could cause a nuclear station to release harmful radioactivity. Communities sometimes protest plans to build a reactor in their neighborhood due to fears about radioactive accidents. Since they produce vast amounts of electricity, reactors need to be located where they can be connected to a grid with pylons and high-voltage wires.

An abandoned nuclear plant located near a body of water.

Reactor types

There are different types of reactors but the most common is the pressurized water reactor (PWR). Over half of all reactors are this design. In a PWR, fission, or atom splitting, takes place in the core and releases nuclear and thermal, or heat, energy. Water, under pressure from coolant pumps, passes through the core in pipes and is warmed by the thermal energy. Entering a heat exchanger, the water's thermal energy passes into water inside a second system of pipes at lower pressure. When the water in this system reaches the boiling point it evaporates into steam. The pressurized steam blasts across the surface of turbines and makes them spin. This is an example of mechanical energy. An attached shaft leads from the turbines to a generator where magnets spin inside wire coils. This creates electrical energy. The electricity is sent along cables into the power grid. Meanwhile, the steam is passed over a cool surface inside a condenser, and turns back into water. This is sent back to the containment building to be turned into steam again by the heat energy of the atomic fission process.

CASE STUDY

Nuclear Power at Sea

Nuclear reactors onboard ships and submarines also heat water to create steam. This drives the ships' propellers and pushes them through the water. Nuclear power allows vessels to remain at sea for long periods without the need to refuel. U.S.S. Nautilus was the first nuclear powered submarine, built by the American navy in 1955. It was followed in 1960 by an aircraft carrier, U.S.S. Enterprise, still in service. The U.S. Navy has logged over 50 years of accident-free nuclear sailing on over 80 nuclear ships.

A Russian nuclear powered submarine

The Reactor

Nuclear reactors are heat engines. The heat, or thermal energy, they harness is used to produce steam. The steam drives turbines which produce electricity. Nuclear fission takes place in the reactor core. Reactors create this energy sequence by using pellets of enriched uranium 235 as fuel. The pellets are packed into long tubes called fuel rods which are lowered into the reactor core. Control rods, holding the elements boron or cadmium, are added to control the speed of fission. They transmit, or pass on, heat.

Heavy Water

Water or graphite, around the fuel rods, slows the fast moving neutrons and prevents them from escaping. Some reactors use **heavy water** as the moderator, or slowing, fluid to control the reaction.

The reactor at the Chernobyl nuclear plant was covered by a dome after the accident.

The Core

As the neutrons bombard, or continuously stream at, the U-235, its atoms split. About two pounds (one kg) of U-235 undergoing fission will produce thermal energy equivalent to burning 2,500 tons (2268 metric tons) of coal. The core is protected inside a heavy steel vessel surrounded by concrete. The concrete may be as thick as three feet (one m). Vessels must be strong enough to withstand high temperatures and radiation surges. Cracks could result in radiation leaks. A water coolant leak could result in the core over heating.

Containment

Vessels must be able to withstand earthquakes, hurricanes, and even crashes of small aircraft. Reactors are outfitted with emergency cooling systems and power supplies. Even if all this failed and the reactor core overheated and melted, the pressure vessel should still be able to contain the radioactive materials.

Chernobyl: Nuclear Nightmare

On April 26, 1986 the world's worst nuclear disaster occurred in the Chernobyl Power Plant in Ukraine. The plant's four reactors were unsafely constructed without containment vessels. A chain reaction went out of control, causing a steam and chemical explosion and fire. Poisonous materials were deposited in water, soil, and on crops. Soon after, 336,000 people were evacuated, never to return. An entire town was abandoned. It is believed that 56 people died at the accident site from radiation and 600,000 more were exposed to radiation. Many of them later developed cancers and thyroid disease and have since died. Hundreds of deformed animals were born.

(above) People had to leave everything behind when they evacuated their homes.

(above) The houses of a village near Chernobyl still exist, but radiation levels prevent people from returning.

(right) A geiger counter measures radioactivity.

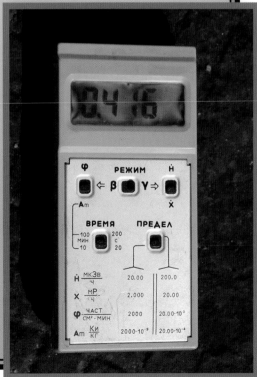

Nuclear Waste

Nuclear waste is the waste product of nuclear power generation. The waste includes radioactive material such as depleted, or used up, uranium, and spent fuel rods. When uranium is used as a fuel in nuclear reactors, it must be enriched. The process of enrichment makes the uranium more radioactive. After 12 to 24 months of use, the uranium inside fuel rods is considered "spent." It can no longer produce the chain reaction needed for energy creation. Spent fuel rods are then pulled out of the core and the reactor is shut down. The rods, which are now nuclear waste, cannot just be thrown out. They are too radioactive and dangerous. Instead, they are placed into cooling pools.

What is a "half-life"?

Most nuclear waste takes a long time to decay, or become non-threatening to life on Earth. Physicists use the term half-life to describe the period of time a decaying substance takes to reduce by one half. They use mathematical formulas to determine the amount of time. For example, if a substance has a half-life of 1,000 years, at the end of that time it will be half as radioactive as it was at the beginning. The half-life of uranium-238 is 4.5 billion years. The half-life of uranium-235 is 704 million years. Radioactive waste is divided into low, intermediate, and high level depending on how much radiation it gives off. Most high-level waste has a relatively short half-life. It is not known how long it will take for all the current nuclear waste to become non-threatening. Estimates range from 10,000 to millions of years.

Waste Disposal

Disposing of nuclear waste raises serious environmental concerns. Reactor waste continues to decay and emit radiation for millions of years. In the 50 years or more since nuclear plants began operating, the waste has mainly been stored at each site. Fuel rods have remained in water pools waiting for a solution to the problem of safe, long-term storage. The water shields the radiation and provides cooling. The pools are surrounded by concrete containers with thick walls and steel linings. After a few years the waste can be transferred to storage casks made of concrete and with air cooling.

Storage Solutions

The big problem with nuclear waste is the radiation danger it poses to wildlife habitats, water systems, and human health. It must be stored for a long time. One solution is storing it deep underground. The Yucca Mountain storage site in Nevada is in a very dry and remote area where storage tunnels are 1640 feet (500 m) deep, and 984 feet (300 m) above the water table. The site is scheduled to open in 2010.

Other Options

In Sweden, scientists coated test canisters containing nuclear waste with copper to make them rust resistant. The canisters were lowered into shafts coated with clay to protect them from running water and earthquakes. Sensors monitor the temperature, bacterial action, water movement, and tension in the rocks. In Finland, a waste disposal site is being built underground. It will hold the waste produced by the four Finnish reactors over 40 years. The site might be operational by 2020.

Nuclear waste must be stored safely away from animal habitats.

Theories for dealing with waste have included disposal in the deep ocean, and in deep space via rockets.

Pros and Cons

Nuclear generating stations produce energy without emitting carbon dioxide, nitrogen oxide, or smog-causing sulphur. They might help nations meet their targets in reducing greenhouse gases that contribute to global warming. Although other renewable resources create energy without causing air pollution, nuclear power is the only source that provides energy on such a massive scale.

A nuclear plant blends into the landscape.

But...

Nuclear power is based on uranium ore, a non-renewable resource. Mining uranium causes water pollution, radioactive dust, and the release of radon, a radioactive gas. Chlorofluorocarbons are chemicals used for the enrichment of uranium. They cause damage to the ozone layer of the atmosphere and contribute to global warming. In the United States, 93 percent of all chlorofluorocarbons used are for uranium enrichment.

The electricity generated in nuclear power plants powers electric appliances, but it is not cheap.

Nuclear Costs

The cost of building a nuclear generating station is high. The process requires special safety standards and skilled engineers, and takes eight to 15 years. Operating a power station requires skilled staff. The cost of electricity from a nuclear plant has been higher overall than electricity from a coal or gas fired plant. New carbon taxes that industries must pay for polluting the atmosphere, may make it more expensive to operate a gas or coal fueled plant. In this case, the cost of nuclear power could be more attractive.

Making the Change

Nuclear plants can produce power efficiently, and people are realizing they do not contribute to global warming as much as fossil fuel-powered plants do.

New Solutions

No new plants have been built in the United States since 1995. Many existing ones will reach the end of their life span in the next 30 years. If nuclear power is going to help meet rising energy demands, new plant construction must take place. This raises issues for governments and citizens about economics and safety.

Future-Tech

In 1999, the U.S. Department of Energy launched a program called Generation IV. Nine countries are participating to develop new, safer types of reactors that produce power more cheaply. Next generation reactors might be gas cooled, water cooled, or fast spectrum. One design is the helium-cooled, Pebble Bed Modular Reactor that contains thousand of balls of uranium and graphite. Since these cannot melt, and degrade slowly, they are much safer than fuel rods. Pebble bed reactors are more efficient than traditional water reactors, and create more thermal energy. Each pebble reactor can produce 120 **megawatts** of electricity in a unit one-tenth the size of current power generating stations.

An old nuclear cooling tower is demolished. New nuclear technology is more efficient than older technology.

Other Designs

Environmental activists press governments to take action to end global warming.

Some Generation IV reactors might be water cooled more safely by having all the main components inside a single vessel. This would overcome the danger of loss of coolant with resultant overheating. Fast spectrum reactors can make new fuel, and make less waste. This decreases the demand for more uranium to be mined.

CASE STUDY

Switching Sides?

Since 1971, members of the environmental organization Greenpeace have campaigned against environmental issues including uranium mining, nuclear testing, and nuclear waste. Recently, Greenpeace founder Patrick Moore has changed his opinion on nuclear power. He points out that 600 coal-fired electrical plants produce 36 percent of greenhouse gas emissions in the United States. Nuclear energy, he says "is the only large-scale, cost-effective energy source that can reduce these emissions while continuing to satisfy a growing demand for power. And these days it can do so safely." Moore believes that wind and solar power are unpredictable, natural gas is expensive, coal is polluting, and resources for creating new hydroelectricity are dwindling. He feels that nuclear power offers the best hope for weaning off fossil fuels.

Timeline

Nuclear power, created by splitting uranium atoms, can create vast amounts of electrical energy. It has the potential to supply much of the world's energy demand.

Knowing their destructive capability, many countries keep a watchful eye on nuclear weapons throughout the world.

1896

Radioactive waves discovered in uranium ore by French scientist, Henri Bequerel.

1908

Hans Geiger and Ernest Rutherford invent the Geiger counter, an instrument still used to measure radiation levels.

1911

Ernest Rutherford discovers that atoms have a nucleus surrounded by electrons. He is known as the father of nuclear science.

1939

Scientists bombard uranium atoms with neutrons and split them apart in a process called nuclear fission.

1945

American planes drop two atomic bombs on Japan that lead to the end of World War II.

1946

The United States creates the Atomic Energy Commission to study peaceful uses of nuclear science and nuclear energy possibilities. This leads to commercial uses of nuclear technology.

1954

The American Navy launches the first nuclear powered submarine, the U.S.S. Nautilus, breaking all records for time and distance traveled under water.

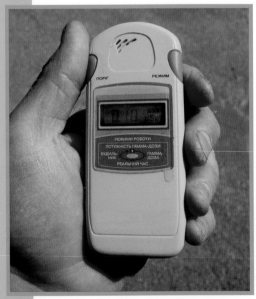

Geiger-Muller detectors measure levels of radiation.

1955

The United Nations Conference on Peaceful Uses of Atomic Energy is held in Switzerland. Two years later, the U.N. creates the International Atomic Energy Agency to promote the peaceful use of nuclear energy and prevent the spread of nuclear weapons.

1956

The world's first commercial nuclear station begins operating at Calder Hall, England.

1957-58

The first nuclear power facility in the USA opens.

1979

At a reactor at Three Mile Island, Pennsylvania, a cooling pump fails. The core overheated and radioactive material escapes from the containment vessel.

1985

At a laboratory in California, scientists use a huge laser called Nova to create nuclear fusion. This produces energy in the same way as the Sun.

1986

An accident at a nuclear plant at Chernobyl, in the Soviet Union, releases clouds of radioactive pollution over Europe, causing deaths, illness, and birth defects.

More than 30 years later, radiation-contaminated ships rust in a river near the Chernobyl nuclear accident. They are not safe for humans to move them.

2000

Over 400 nuclear power stations exist in 31 countries. France gets three-quarters of its energy from nuclear sources and the United States gets about one-fifth.

2005

The U.S. government awards subsidies to the nuclear power industry totaling $20 billion. The following year, the U.K. government relaxes planning laws to speed up the construction of new nuclear plants.

Nuclear power is one alternative to carbon-based fuels, but waste disposal issues makes it less safe than other alternatives such as wind power.

Glossary

atmosphere An envelope of protective gases that surround Earth and absorb the Sun's harmful rays

atom he basic unit of matter, the substance that all objects are made of

chemical A substance with a specific composition. Petrochemicals are chemicals made from petroleum, or oil and gas

compression Intense pressure that reduces volume

consumption Using something up, such as a resource

developing nations Poorer agricultural countries that are attempting to become more advanced economically and socially

electrometer An instrument for measuring electrical potential

element One of more than 100 substances that cannot be broken down into simpler substances

enrichment To increase something and make it more powerful or explosive

finite Having limits or bounds

fossil fuels Fuels found in Earth's crust that are non-renewable sources of energy

greenhouse gases Gases in the atmosphere that absorb heat from Earth's surface

heavy water Water with changed molecules, which is used as a moderator, or something to slow neutrons, in nuclear reactors

infinite Something limitless or endless

matter Anything of physical substance

megawatts Units used to measure electricity

ore Mineral bearing rock

petrochemical Substances made from refined and processed petroleum, or oil and gas

physicist A scientist who studies the nature and properties of matter and energy

physics A field of science that studies the nature and properties of energy and matter including heat, light, sound, electricity, and other subjects

radioactive waste Waste containing radioactive material; it is often the result of generating nuclear energy

theory An idea or system of ideas intended to explain something

turbines Machines for producing power that use wheels or rotors with vanes that revolve with the fast-moving flow of water, steam, gas, or air

watersheds An area drained by a river, or an area separated by flowing waters where many animals and waterfowl make their home

Index